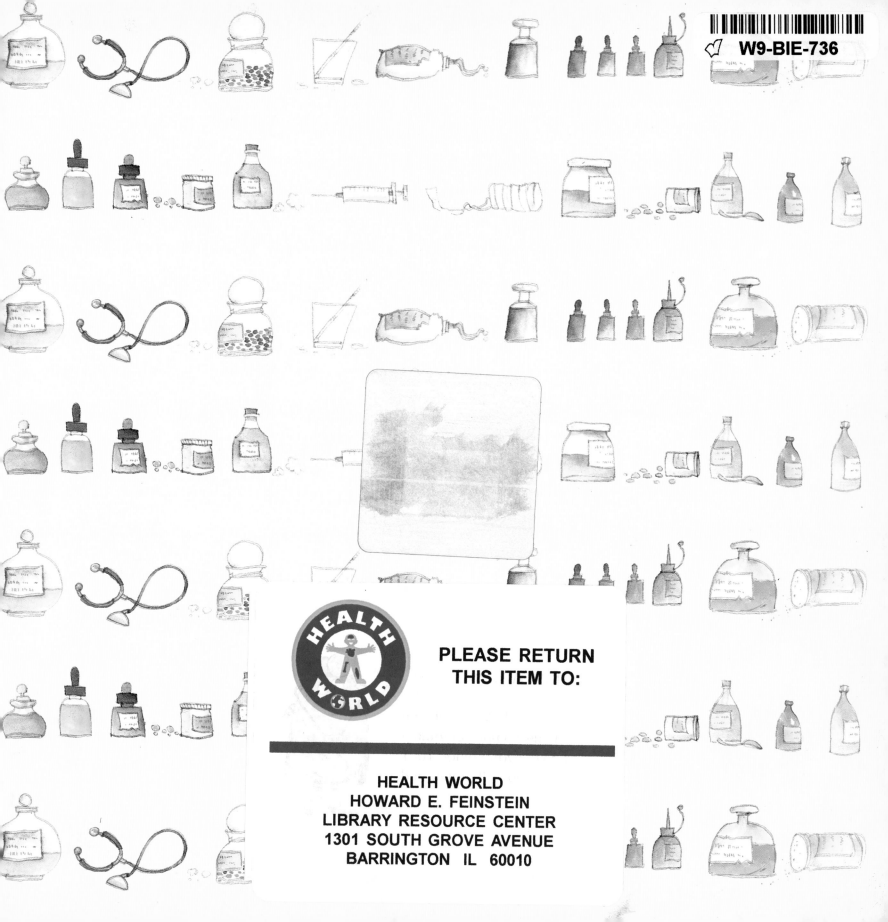

Dr. Dog

Babette Cole

Alfred A. Knopf
New York · Toronto

This is the Gumboyle family.

And this is their dog. He is a doctor.

Dr. Dog went to
a conference in
Brazil to give a talk
about bone marrow.

While he was away, Granddad and the Gumboyle children got ill.

"We'd better get him back!" said Ma Gumboyle.

So they sent a message to Brazil. . .

. . . and Dr. Dog came home.

Kurt Gumboyle had been secretly smoking in the
bicycle shed. He had a wicked cough.
"It's not good to smoke,"
said Dr. Dog.

"These spongy things inside our chests are called lungs. They are our breathing machines.

Smoke fills them up with dirty tar. Then they don't work properly, and so we cough."

Gerty Gumboyle had not been wearing her raincoat and hat.

She caught a cold and got a sore throat.

The germs attacked her tonsils.

"She's got tonsillitis," said Dr. Dog.

"I will have to operate!"

So he took them out!

Kev Gumboyle was scratching his head like mad.

"He's got nits!" said Dr. Dog.
"These are eggs laid
by little insects
called lice.

This is one!
They live in
your hair!"

He plastered Kev's hair with smelly shampoo to kill the lice, and Kev had to wear it all day at school.

"Never swap combs and brushes with anyone!" said Dr. Dog.

Ha Ha!

Ha!

Baby Gumboyle did not wash his hands
after going to the toilet.
Then he sucked his thumb.

And he let other children
stick their fingers up
his nose.

So he got a tummy ache.

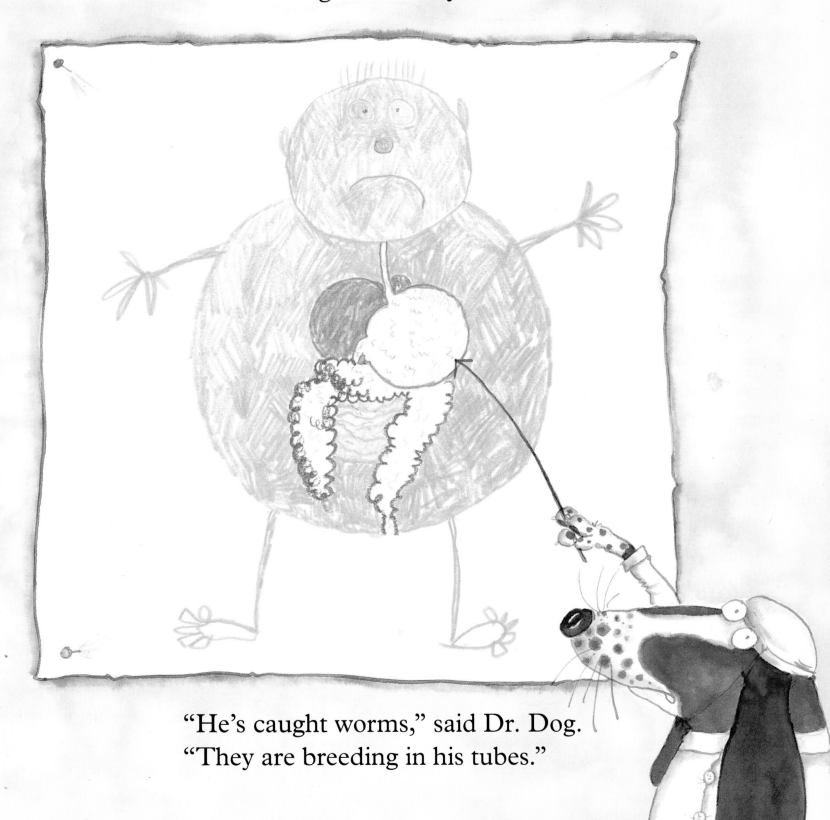

"He's caught worms," said Dr. Dog.
"They are breeding in his tubes."

"The worms wriggle inside you until they reach your bottom. There they lay itchy little eggs.

If you scratch your bum, the eggs go under your fingernails."

"Sucking your thumb makes the eggs go back into your tummy, where they hatch into more worms again!

Never scratch your bum and suck your thumb!" said Dr. Dog.

Fiona Gumboyle felt dizzy.

"It's all those cartwheels she's been turning!" laughed her parents.

"Nonsense," growled Dr. Dog. "She's got an earache."

"There are tiny bones inside our ears that help us balance. An earache can affect these and make us dizzy."

Dr. Dog gave her some pills.

Granddad had been eating too many baked beans
and drinking too much beer.
"He's got terrible wind!" said Dr. Dog.

"Here's a picture of your inside tubes.

Beer and baked beans make gases in your tummy. The only way they can escape is to blast out of your bottom!"

"It's *disgusting*," Dr. Dog told Ma and Pa Gumboyle. "If you don't take better care of your family, there will be a serious accident."

"So what!" said the Gumboyles. "We've got you to look after us, haven't we?"

Meanwhile, Granddad's dangerous gases were building up and . . .

. . . he farted so hard he blew the roof right off the house!

"Told you so," said Dr. Dog.

Once the roof had been put back and he had made everyone better, Dr. Dog felt ill himself.

"You're suffering from stress, Dog," said his doctor.
"What you need is a holiday away from that pesky family."

"Just what the doctor ordered," said Dr. Dog.
"They'll never find me here!"

"Oh, no!" said Dr. Dog.

Copyright © 1994 by Babette Cole. All rights reserved under International and Pan-American Copyright Conventions.
Published in the United States by Alfred A. Knopf, Inc., New York, and simultaneously in Canada by Random House of Canada
Limited, Toronto. Distributed by Random House, Inc., New York. Published in Great Britain in 1994 by Jonathan Cape
Limited. Manufactured in Italy 10 9 8 7 6 5 4 3 2 1

Library of Congress Cataloging-in-Publication Data
Cole, Babette. Dr. Dog / by Babette Cole. p. cm.
Summary: The Gumboyle family learns important tips on health care and hygiene from their family dog, who is also a doctor.
ISBN 0-679-86720-1
1. Hygiene—Juvenile literature. 2. Health behavior—Juvenile literature. [1. Health. 2. Cleanliness. 3. Grooming.]
I. Title. II. Title: Dr. Dog. RA777.C65 1994 613'.4'083—dc20 93-51077